The Concerned Beauty and
Barber Professionals'

Guide to
Thrive and Survive

Health, Safety and Longevity in
Salons and Barbershops

TAMARA JOHNSON-SHEALEY

DEDICATION

I dedicate this book to every client that gave me the opportunity and the pleasure of serving them. I appreciate all that serving you taught me.

My work as a Licensed Professional was to ensure your health and safety. I took that very seriously and that was always my #1 concern.

CONTENTS

Acknowledgments   i

1   Introduction   1

2   Before: Look Around, What Did Your Clients See?   4

3   Before: What Did Your Clients Smell?   8

4   Before: What Did Your Clients Feel?   10

5   Now: What Should We Do?   13

6   Now: What Else Can We Do?   20

7   Keys to Longevity   23

8   Now, Let's Get Back to Work   27

ACKNOWLEDGMENTS

I want to thank GOD for blessing me with my talents, my gifts, my abilities and giving me the honor of being the mother of my two wonderful sons…. I Love You Keon and Deven!

I want to thank my ex-husband who did not understand any of what I was doing but held it down as best he could… Thank You!

I want to thank my little sister who is the bossiest person I know, Tawanna Johnson-Blake. I want to thank my spiritual sisters, Joan Bell-Carroll, Vickie Turner, Cheryl Holmes, Nataki Ervin, Nefertiti Nzinga, Latisha Bell, Keisha White and April West for always being just a phone call away… I Love Y'all!

Last but certainly not least, I want to thank the Members of The Concerned Beauty and Barber Professionals/Politics Beauty Barber for believing in our organizational efforts when so many Professionals did not. I want to thank you for making health and safety your #1 concern before anything forced you to do it. Thank you for maintaining the integrity of our industry and your commitment to health and safety.

CHAPTER 1
INTRODUCTION

Professionals, I know your time is valuable so thank you for taking the time to read this book. This will be a short read that will pack a powerful punch....

I wrote this book because I know how wonderfully magical the relationship is between beauty and barber professionals and clients. We are their therapist, confidants, friends and in some cases, we become like extended family. Our clients tell us their secrets; we watch their families grow and we are even there for them in death and divorce. Sometimes we know more about our clients than their own families. However, as magical as this relationship is, it blurs the lines between "client and professional". Our clients are relaxed and comfortable, and we are relaxed and comfortable too. Professionals, it is at this very intersection where practicing proper health and safety goes out the window.

This year, 2020, is a wake-up call for beauty and barber professionals. Health and safety practices must be reintroduced, reemphasized and reinforced if the beauty and barber industry intends to thrive and survive. This wake-up call for beauty and barber professionals and the mandatory and voluntary closing of salons and barbershops and the stifling of our entire industry is something we should never want to see again.

Clients trust us but when they return to our salons and barbershops to receive services, they will be expecting things to have changed, whether they say it or not. They will be expecting Professionals to take their health and safety much more seriously. They will be expecting new protocols, new procedures and a more professional attitude in the way you provide services and in the way you conduct your business. Trust me, that magical relationship will be severed if clients don't see a change and see that change consistently.

Therefore Professionals, it is time to get it right. Your opportunity to hit the reset button and rebuild your business on what this profession and what your license is built upon, and that is protecting the health and safety of the clients you serve. No longer are the days that clients will "trust" that you are keeping them safe, you will have to prove it. They will need to SEE you do it. Your skills and talents will no longer define you as a "professional". Your ability to exemplify the highest health and safety practices, at all times, is what will be the standard of "professionalism" not necessarily, how good you can make them look.

Beauty and Barber Professionals, share this book with your fellow professionals. This is our time to thrive, but in order for that to happen we must reintroduce, reemphasize and reinforce our health and safety practices in our salons and barbershops. But, before we dive into how to thrive, let's address the many aspects of our salon and barbershop culture that we must change first:

CHAPTER 2
BEFORE: LOOK AROUND, WHAT DID YOUR CLIENTS SEE?

Professionals, SMDH.... I am embarrassed by some in my industry. Some of our workspaces, our salons and our barbershops were a mess, a hot mess. Many looked like someone threw a bomb inside and blew them up. Stuff was just everywhere, dirty and cluttered. Yes, I said it and guess what, clients saw it too. Look around, what did your clients see? Your clients saw trash cans that needed to be emptied. They saw your personal belongings. They saw your food, your food containers, your water bottles, your car keys on your station. They saw that you have no sense of organization. They saw the products with the price tags still on them and you wondered why they wouldn't pay more for your services? Why would they when they can go buy the same products and pay what you pay?

Your clients saw those dirty baseboards that you have never cleaned. They saw walls that hadn't been painted since you opened 5 years ago. They saw spots and stains on your floor because you hardly ever mopped. They saw all the stains on the towels that you kept washing over and over again, so much so the towels were flimsy and falling apart. Clients saw the dust on the ceiling fan that you wouldn't take 5 minutes to clean. Yes, that ceiling fan that keeps circulating dust everywhere in the room. Look around, what did your clients see?

Clients saw that caked up dirt on those blinds and those dirty windows. Clients saw that front door that you wouldn't even take a moment and wipe the fingerprints off. Clients barely wanted to use your bathroom. It's dark, it's dingy and it smells funny. The toilet ain't clean and somebody pee'd on the floor. The sink is dirty and nobody has even thought to check the bathroom or even tried to keep it clean. And yes, the trash is running over in there too. Clients saw everything!

Your clients were even looking at you too. Yes, they like you, but you can believe they are looking at you from head-to-toe. They noticed that you needed a haircut and they noticed whatever that was underneath your nails. They noticed that rash on your bottom lip. They noticed that your individual lashes were missing some hairs. They noticed your entire outfit and guess what, they smell you too. (But let's not talk about body odor.) Oh, but your breath, they can smell that too. They are "paying" attention to your every detail and honestly, that is part of what they are "paying" for...

Your clients saw everything. Wait, did you drop that comb or that implement on the floor, wipe it off on your smock, and use it on them? Did you put it back in your drawer to use on someone else? No, you didn't do that. (Yes, you did.) When was the last time you even washed that cape that you draped over them? Heck, when was the last time you even washed your own smock? Can you use some better towels please?

Professionals, I know that in your salon or your barbershop you can't always control or influence the areas outside of your workstation, however, it is your professional responsibility to try. For example: When you drive into your parking lot, look around for trash or anything unsightly on the ground and if you see it, pick it up. If the entrance to your business is bland and boring, purchase a potted plant and put it at the front door. If there needs to be a little painting done to your workspace, take the initiative and just do it. Your place of business is a reflection of you and your clients will appreciate it. Be mindful of what your clients saw and be intentional about what they will see when they return.

CHAPTER 3
BEFORE: WHAT DID YOUR CLIENTS SMELL?

Professionals, what is that smell in your salon or in your barbershop? Clients opened the door and they were immediately hit with it. What is that smell? Is it the combination of chemicals from all the products that you use? What are you misting? What are you spraying? What is that smell when you are flat ironing? What is causing that smell? Nail Techs, what are you mixing and applying? Estheticians, why does that lash glue smell funny? Wait, is that your lunch they smell too? Did you put something in the microwave that you shouldn't have?

Clients smell everything. And sadly, we, beauty and barber professionals, weren't taught about proper ventilation, air quality or air flow. We don't know much about the chemicals in the air inside of our salons and barbershops and the chemical combinations that are toxic. But we do know that after days and days and years and years of being exposed to "something" in our salons and barbershops, "something" is wreaking havoc on our health.

Yes, ventilation can be expensive but ventilation is necessary. Not only will proper ventilation address the concerns of the day-to-day air quality in our salons and barbershops, but it will also address the dire need to keep the air in our salons and barbershops as clean as possible. Investing in ventilation would build client confidence and demonstrate that we are going above and beyond to keep them safe.

CHAPTER 4
BEFORE: WHAT DID YOUR CLIENTS FEEL?

Professionals, every day should be a good day in the salon and barbershop. It doesn't matter what is going on in your life and not to be insensitive to the fact that Professionals are human and we have many challenges, but when you show up to work, "show up to work". When you cross the threshold to your salon or barbershop, as the old folks would say, "leave everything at the door". Do not bring your personal life to your workplace. Professionals, if things are that bad, and there may be a time when things are that bad, reschedule your clients and get yourself together. Don't subject your clients to what you are going through.

When your clients come to see you, they deserve your

undivided attention and your job is to set the mood, not kill the mood. Professionals, check your emotions so that you can meet your client's needs. Get your feelings out of the way. Your clients come to you for them, not for you. If they had a rough day, they may just want to relax. If your client is feeling down and need a shoulder to lean on, that is a part of your job. If they are happy, you get a chance to be even happier with them. Each client will bring you a different mood and your job is to "positively meet them wherever they are".

Here are some tips: When your client comes in the door, greet them immediately. (You should have already checked your emotions and you should be receptive to how your client is feeling. By checking your emotions, you now have the space to discern what your client is feeling, even if they don't tell you.) Did the client give you a warm, friendly smile? Did your client look like they had a hard day and just needed to relax? Was your client seemingly bothered by something or in a bad mood? At that very moment, your job is to discern where your client is emotionally so that you can "positively meet them wherever they are".

What does "positively meet them wherever they are" actually mean? It means, you make your clients experience the best you can. If your client is in a good mood, that is great! Join in and enjoy the positive energy flow that is around you. This positive energy could carry you throughout your entire day and when the next client comes and if they are not in a great mood, you have your own good energy stored up. Be empathetic and feel what your clients are feeling but do as much as you can to turn bad energy into good energy. It's easy, just remember how much you enjoy your work. Share your good energy with your clients and keep filling yourself with good energy throughout the day.

Professionals, listen with your heart. Your job is to offer positive thoughts and positive energy in response. Remember, you should have some good energy stored up from other clients and the good energy that you brought into work with you. Professionals, we are special people, chosen to make others look good and feel good. This is our gift as beauty and barber professionals. We carry energy and we have the ability to affect moods and attitudes. We are gifted to make our clients feel good inside and out. This is naturally who we are...

CHAPTER 5
NOW: WHAT SHOULD WE DO?

No one is actually "safe" in our salons and barbershops and now in 2020, that is crystal clear. However, the good news is that the foundation of our industry is built on health and safety and Beauty and Barber Professionals have been trained for such a time as this.

Professionals, now more than ever before, we must be diligent and intentional in our health and safety practices. Our problem with practicing health and safety prior was, we had either forgotten how to do most of what we were taught, or we were too busy, or some of us were just too lazy. Nevertheless, here is how we should build upon our current practices when we return to work:

- **Sanitize, Disinfect and Sterilize** – Yes, we know to sanitize and disinfect our work areas, our tools and our implements **but** not many of us have ever sterilized anything. Sterilization is the complete elimination of all microbial life, including spores and investing in an autoclave could not only increase client confidence but could yield some extra profits, as most clients won't mind paying a bit more to be safe. Our clients must now see and know that we are going above and beyond. They must see you sanitize and disinfect your station (and your client chair), the shampoo bowls, the dryers and EVERYTHING they would come in contact with…. Clients need to see and know that everything is clean and if they don't physically see you clean, create a protocol, a system that signals to your client that this area, this tool, this implement has been cleaned and disinfected just for them. (Here is an idea, create a sign that says, "This Area Has Been Sanitized and Disinfected" and place it in the area after you have cleaned.) Also, for each client, you could package tools and implements in individual packets or bags. This would be a great indicator to your clients that the tools and/or implements that you are using are sanitized and disinfected.

- **Good Ole Fashion Handwashing or Using Hand Sanitizer** – Yes, we know to thoroughly wash our hands for 20 seconds or to use hand sanitizer between our clients **but** how many Professionals were actually doing this? Don't answer that... Washing our hands or using hand sanitizer between every client is an absolute must. (In addition, Professionals, you should wash or use hand sanitizer on your forearm, up to and including your elbow, if you are wearing a short sleeve shirt.)

- **Wearing Gloves** – Yes, we know to wear gloves, however, most professionals wear gloves with chemical services or when we "feel" we should, based on what we see with each individual client. Wearing gloves is not a standard practice for the entirety of our services but it should be. I know, I know, gloves get in the way, right? You can't "feel" what you are doing with that barrier between you and the client. Well Professionals, now it is time to **learn** how to render that same great service wearing gloves or at minimum, wearing gloves until you have cleaned the skin, scalp or hair. For example:

  o Cosmetologist, when a client sits in your chair, don't touch the client's hair or skin without gloves. (If you don't wear gloves for the entirety of the service, shampoo the hair and cleanse the scalp and the skin that you will be touching before removing the gloves and exposing yourself.)

- o Barbers, if you are not shampooing your client's hair or beard and cleansing the client's scalp or skin, you should wear gloves for the entire service.
- o Nail Techs, you are constantly touching the client's skin, therefore, you should wear gloves as a standard practice for the entire service.
- o Esthetician, you are constantly touching the skin, therefore, you should wear gloves as a standard practice for the entire service.

Having a negative feeling about the "fit and feel" of gloves should have no bearing on health and safety. We are Professionals and we can still render great services, even in gloves. We just have to learn how to do it.

- **Wear a Mask** – Yes, we should now wear a mask. This is our new normal and the N95 is recommended for the best protection. The N95 mask will protect you from VIRUSES, germs and dust. Professionals should wear the N95 during the entire service. There is no such thing as social distancing in the beauty and barber industry. We need to wear a mask and our clients need to wear a mask too. Professionals, consider providing a disposable mask to your clients if they don't come in with their own mask. This would be extra protection for both you and your client. (I would not encourage re-usable, washable face mask. You don't need the added responsibility of handling a mask that could possibly be contaminated.)

- **Reusing Capes** – Yes, a clean, washed cape for every client. No more re-using of the same cape client after client. Every client needs a clean, washed cape when they sit in your chair.

- **Take Your Temperature and Your Client's Temperature** – Yes, take your temperature prior to the beginning of your shift, halfway through your shift and at the end of your shift. Monitor your body in ways that you have never done before. Be sure to stay hydrated. (DO NOT DRINK AT YOUR STATION. Professionally we should not be doing this anyway and in 2020, it is obvious why.) If you feel out of the ordinary, stop and take care of yourself. Professionals, we are notorious for pushing through when we are not well. Please, stop working when you are not feeling well and take care of yourself.

Yes, take your client's temperature too because taking your client's temperature could save your career. For example, what if a client became sick and died after a visit with you and your local health officials found that your salon was among the last places that the client visited? How would you prove that you and your salon were not the culprit? Well, here is how: **Take your client's temperature when they enter your salon, of course wear your mask and gloves, and create a standard form with the date, time and temperature reading and have the client sign the form.** You could then prove, with your client's signature, that your client did not have a temperature when they came into your salon for their service. This could validate why you proceeded with the service and you could avoid a lawsuit... Look, I know this might seem far-fetched, but this may be your only protection from a lawsuit that could end your career and wreck your life.

You can choose to adopt temperature reading practices or not, but this book is written as a guide to help you thrive and survive. (If you choose to adopt this practice, purchase a forehead thermometer and you won't have to touch the client. It reads the heat waves as you wave the thermometer across the client's forehead.) Professionals, your clients will appreciate the heightened concern for their health and safety. Remember a normal temperature reading ranges around 98.6 degrees Fahrenheit (37 degrees Celsius).

CHAPTER 6
NOW: WHAT ELSE CAN WE DO?

Glad you asked...

- **Additional Practices:**
    - ○ **Face Shields** – There is no such thing as too much protection and having a barrier to completely cover your face should be considered.
    - ○ **Ventilation** – Invest in a ventilation system (whole salon or portable) or at minimum opening a door and/or using a ceiling fan for clean air flow.
    - ○ **Designated Work Clothes** – Invest in a standard uniform or have designated work clothes that you wear to the salon or barbershop. These clothes should be taken off immediately when you arrive

home and contained and washed separately from your personal laundry. You don't want to expose yourself or your family to anything that you might have been exposed to at the salon or barbershop.

o **Appointment Only** – Unless you are able to stop and make sure every walk in is not contagious AND you can ensure 6ft of safe distancing, accepting walk ins should be reconsidered.

o **Space and Pace Yourself** – No longer should you stack your client book and schedule clients too closely. Space your client appointments to allow yourself time to properly sanitize and disinfect between each client. (Raise your prices to accommodate for this extra time. Clients will gladly pay for it.)

o **Rearrange the Salon/Barbershop** - Clients now need 6ft of personal distance from other clients. Make sure your hair dryers are spaced accordingly. You probably won't be able to move shampoo bowls and therefore, I recommend rotating the use of the shampoo bowls. For example, if you have 4 shampoo bowls, maybe use bowls 1 and 3 and then use bowls 2 and

4. Create a system that offers the 6ft of safe distancing between clients and professionals.   Also,   if   the salon/barbershop has several stations and you cannot move the stations further apart for safe distancing, consider rotating the days that Professionals work. For example, if your barbershop has 6 Barbers. Consider 3 of them working on Tuesday with safe distancing, and the next 3 working on Wednesday with safe distancing. Then start the rotation over again with the first 3 Barbers working again on Thursday. This type of rotating schedule could work really well for social distancing and for Professionals who have raised their prices to accommodate for the new health and safety practices. Professionals could be making the same great money but working less hours.

○   **Installation of a Hand Sanitizing Station at the Door** – Accessibility to hand sanitizer would encourage usage. Install a hand sanitizing station at the door or place large bottles of hand sanitizer around the salon or barbershop.

CHAPTER 7
KEYS TO LONGEVITY

I provided services for 18 years. I had a great career in our industry, and I practiced most of what I shared in this book. These practices allowed me to thrive, survive and have longevity in our industry and I know that these practices will work for you too.

I know, I promised you a quick read, so I will get straight to the point. Here are my 20 Keys to Longevity:

1. **Consultation with Every Client** – Know as much as you can about your client to provide them with the best possible service.
2. **Great Customer Service** – You should always be friendly, upbeat and happy.

3. **Know Your Clients' Name** – Learn it and don't forget it.

4. **Consistent Hours of Operation** – Work by a schedule and stick to it.

5. **Stay in One Location** – Find a location and stay. Avoid moving. Clients won't always follow you.

6. **Consistent Product Line** – Find a product line and stick with it. Don't use multiple or random products on your clients.

7. **Talking Politics and Religion** – I won't tell you not to do it BUT be very careful.

8. **Your Clients Are Your Clients** – Your clients become close friends and like family BUT remember to keep that client relationship first if you want to maintain that stream of income.

9. **Keep It Professional** – Remember this is your career!

10. **Be a Good Listener** – Let the client talk. Focus on doing your best work.

11. **Be Available** – If your client text or call be sure to return the text or call within a reasonable amount of time. It is best to establish a time(s), preferably within the same day, to return calls and texts.

12. **Appointment Reminders** – Clients sometimes forget, and a reminder

would help clients to remember. Reminders would also help make sure you are not losing revenue.

13. **Professional Message on Voicemail** – Need I say more?...

14. **Clean, Neat Work Area** – Make the right impression.

15. **Your Towels** – Please be mindful if there are stains, rips and/or tears in your towels. Don't use those towels on your clients. Buy LOTS of towels and factor the time it takes to wash towels, or the cost associated with paying for a laundry service into your service price. Your clients will understand.

16. **Prices on Your Bottles** – Your clients should never see sticker prices on your products.

17. **Using Products from BIG containers** – Use smaller jars and containers. Never let clients see you using products from BIG containers. Presentation is so important.

18. **Rushing Through Services** – Slow down. Clients do not like to feel rushed.

19. **Be True to Yourself** – Specialize in services that speak to who you are. Don't follow trends. Just be you.

20. **Clean the Bathroom** – Make sure that your bathroom is ALWAYS clean. Check it frequently.

CHAPTER 8
NOW, LET'S GET BACK TO WORK

This year, 2020, is a wake-up call for beauty and barber professionals and the entire beauty and barber industry. For far too long, health and safety has taken a backburner to professionals who want to be celebrities in the industry, a mindset that has gotten professionals totally off course. Our priorities, as professionals, have truly been in the wrong place.

And while we were willfully distracted with "celebritism", the beauty and barber industry has been plagued with deregulation, the greed of corporate profit, the lowering of our professional standards and the devaluing of our professional license. This year was definitely a wake-up call and I hope that now Professionals are "woke". The lives of our clients are literally in our hands and performing services could be a matter of life and death, including our own.

Professionals, now is our time to reclaim our industry and demand higher standards, both at the state and federal level. No longer can and no longer will deregulation win. Health and safety in the Beauty and Barber Industry is back at the forefront, where it rightfully belongs.

Professionals, we will thrive and survive and everything in this guide should be implemented and built upon to bring integrity back to our industry and to our profession. Share this information with fellow Beauty and Barber Professionals and join our organization, **The Concerned Beauty and Barber Professional / Politics Beauty and Barber**, www.TheCBBP.org/joinus. We are doing the work...

Now, take this guide, strictly adhere to it and let's get back to work!

ABOUT
TAMARA JOHNSON-SHEALEY

Tamara is the Founder and President of The Concerned Beauty and Barber Professionals, an organization that addresses the need to protect the health and safety of Licensed Beauty and Barber Professionals and the clients they serve... www.TheCBBP.org

Tamara is the Founder and Senior Advocate of Politics Beauty and Barber, an organization that works to strengthen the professional license of the beauty and barber industry and encourage Licensed Beauty and Barber Professionals to engage in the political process. Tamara tracks, monitors and addresses policy nationwide that affects the beauty and barber industry... www.PoliticsBeautyBarber.org

Tamara is also a 2020 Candidate for the United States Senate (Georgia), with an agenda that includes addressing the need for national health and safety standards in the Beauty and Barber Industry... www.TamaraForGeorgia.com

Made in the USA
Middletown, DE
19 April 2020